E

THE JOURNEY OF A K   AND
HOMELESS VETERANS

BY LYNETTE LOOMIS
ILLUSTRATIONS BY MEG SPENCER

Published by Starry Night Publishing.Com

Rochester, New York

Copyright 2016 Lynette Loomis

Dedication

Dedicated to our veterans, their families,
the staff and volunteers who serve them,
and all the dogs who enrich our lives.

Lynette Loomis

Contents

Dedication 3
Foreword..7
PART ONE — The Veterans 9
  Marv Patterson 11
  M., Small Business Owner...15
  Jake 17
  Rodney 21
  Nick...23
  Cathy, Nick's Mom..27
  Gary...29
  Matt and His Kids 31
  Amy, Military Wife of a Solider with Multiple Deployments.............33
PART TWO — Hans 35
  Me as a Pup...37
  On the Road Again...39
  Take Me for a Ride in the Car...or Truck..43
  Partying and Sports Bars..47
  After All, I'm Still a Puppy...49
  The Groomer..51
  Felix the Cat..53
  Glen...57
  Patrick 59
  Daniel..61
  Andy..63
  Shane...65
  My First Birthday..67
  Epilogue 69
Appendix...71
  Hans' and Amy's Cookies 71
  No, Hans, No..72
  Depression and Suicide 73
Acknowledgments 75

Lynette Loomis

Foreword

These are the experiences of recent veterans returning to civilian life and involved with Veterans Outreach Center (VOC) in Rochester, NY. Post deployment, these veterans faced challenges that could include unemployment, anger, grief, substance abuse, legal problems and mental health issues. Some, if not many, dealt with physical or moral pain.

The men and the dog in this book are real. They all experienced loneliness, homelessness and, sometimes, hopelessness. In Part One, the short vignettes were told directly to the author by seven veterans, a military spouse and a mother of a veteran. All volunteered to participate in this book in the hope that the significant re-entry challenges faced by some men would shed light onto the adjustment issues of many veterans.

Part Two begins in late 2015 when a black lab puppy was rescued from a kill shelter in the South and brought to New York State. He was named Hans. It was hoped that if the puppy had the right temperament and training, he could offer friendship, comfort and laughter to veterans. This included the men in VOC's residential homes, Richards House and Otto House, and in VOC's job training and counseling programs. Part Two offers the stories of these men as told to Hans, in the presence of the author. The unique perspective of Hans offers humor and a sense of hopefulness.

It is intended that those who read this book will have a better understanding of our veterans and the challenges they face. We encourage our readers to listen to veterans with an open mind and to give them reason to hope that they can have a positive future when they return home.

PART ONE
The Veterans

Lynette Loomis

Marv Patterson, U.S. Army Reserves;
Investigator, Rochester City Police Department;
Board Member, Veterans Outreach Center

Enlist? With a father, grandfather, cousins and several uncles all veterans, it almost seemed like it was in my blood to enlist when I was 18. It was a calling. It never occurred to me to do otherwise. After high school, I attempted college, per my father's advice, but I was not interested in more schoolwork at that time. I enlisted in the U.S. Army and went to Boot Camp in 1985, knowing my family felt proud that I was following in the footsteps of the men for whom we felt so much respect.

I have had many great experiences during my military career, especially my first active duty station. My first duty station was Schofield Barracks, Hawaii, as a Combat Engineer. This was the 25th ID and a specialized light infantry division. My main duties were bridge construction, mine laying, minesweeping, obstacle clearing and demolitions. Our main transportation was either our "legs" or air insertion by helicopter. Very rarely did we rely on trucks or armored vehicles. The tropical and mountainous terrain in Hawaii was not suitable for that kind of heavy equipment.

My unit deployed to South Korea, Operation Team Spirit, to train with the South Korean Army during war-gaming exercises against the threat of North Korea. Our militaries shared knowledge of light and heavy infantry tactics and various demolition techniques. We also deployed to Japan. Operation Orient Shield was similar to the preparation for war with North Korea. When I deployed to Panama, I had the opportunity to attend Jungle School at Ft. Sherman, and was on standby due to civil unrest within Panama's cities.

When my initial active duty tour ended in 1988, I remained in the Ready Reserves (now age 22) and joined the Monroe County Sheriff's Department, full-time Road Patrol. I served there for two years and then transferred to the Rochester Police Department, in Rochester, New York. After 9/11, in October 2002, I deployed to Afghanistan for Operation Enduring Freedom. It was a very different experience on this deployment, because our nation was at war, and we knew our purpose.

I wanted to make a difference; I was assigned to the Civil Affairs Team (CA-T). We helped the local community rebuild their infrastructure, consisting of their schools, stores, public facilities and a community center. One of the fortunate differences between me and other Reservists was that I was a police officer within my community and I was accustomed to handling weapons on a daily basis. Due to my civilian profession, I was used to living and dealing with the stress of potential dangers. I believe it was harder on the soldiers who had been bankers and teachers during the week and drilling Reservists on the weekends. This was a different scenario for them, thrust into a wartime situation.

To keep our sanity, we still rehearsed war games and also participated in a variety of sports. Our unit played soccer and volleyball with local citizens, which allowed them to see we were there to help them fight for democracy. It also showed them we had a competitive and fun side in our down time. By the time we arrived "in country," many of the Taliban fighters had retreated into their communities and reintegrated themselves amongst the local population. This was unnerving because we could not easily identify the enemy forces. They walked and lived amongst us and were not identifiable.

We knew we were in harm's way, at all times, but managed to maintain our situational awareness. Our Host Nation Afghan Guards, who guarded our "safe house," made it a point to recruit their own family members and lifelong friends to protect us. They did this because they wanted people they knew they could trust.

During the nine months I was there, I saw the toll it took on other troops. They missed their families, and wanted to stay alive so they could return home and be a dad or mom, a brother or sister, or a son or daughter. They missed the certainty of a safe environment, what they were accustomed to in their own communities, in the U.S.

Many of the guys were cautious about certain sounds, what they meant, either harmless or life threatening. Others felt concerned over missing important family events and job opportunities, and not being included or remembered. Some men wondered how they would ever be able to explain how they were feeling and what they had experienced when they returned home. And some of the guys were dealing with domestic issues, prior to deployment, and feared they would not have a home when they returned.

I was very blessed to have a family that was eager to see me. A good friend cared for my dog; another friend painted my motorcycle while I was away. My realtor stayed connected with me, via email, helping me to find a new home while I was going through a divorce. I had a career waiting for me when I returned and old friends to see. Not everyone had the same support system, which helped me remain level during my stressful times.

In two separate incidents, I lost two friends, not to combat- related situations. Both men committed suicide. One lived in Rochester and the other in Utah. I don't know if either of them ever reached out to a non-profit, veteran-centric place, such as Veterans Outreach Center. It feels unforgiveable that these men, and many others, faced so many dangers in the military, that their depression was so great. The feeling of hopelessness must have been so intense, that the taking of their lives seemed like the only possible solution.

Once I was given the opportunity to join the board of VOC, I did not hesitate. It is my hope that more communities will duplicate what

Rochester has created and sustained for more than 40 years. None of us wishes to lose another "battle buddy."

M., Small Business Owner

In a family of seven kids and as the only boy, there was a lot of pressure to decide what I wanted to do with my life, especially from my dad. I knew I needed structure, and the recruiter was pretty good in sales. I signed up with the Marines as a tank engineer and served four years' active duty and another four in inactive duty.

Boot Camp was not that difficult for me as I had played sports and worked out a lot. I wouldn't say it was fun, but it was manageable. The most challenging part for me was people telling me what to do all the time, more so than even teachers, coaches or my parents. That took an adjustment; I had to adapt. I will say I got in a few scrapes with a couple of guys; we all had "our muscles on." The guys I met in Boot Camp will be in my life forever.

I was in the Persian Gulf for six months in a combat tank. I guess they placed us single guys in the front because the military figured that if we got blown up from a land mine, it would be less of a loss than a guy with a wife and kids. Being in this conflict was different for us than it was for troops in earlier conflicts where they were cut off from home for months, or even years. We could send tapes back and forth, and once in a while we could call home. That calmed everyone down at home, to know we were OK.

My injury wasn't because of enemy fire; it wasn't even friendly fire. One of our own tanks backed into me because the guy wasn't paying attention and pinned me to the back of it. There are some things I can't do: certain exercises, etc. Compared to what some guys have experienced, it's all good.

15

When I came home, I had friends and family to greet me at the airport. That's not the case for some guys who have no one. My grandfather opened up for the first time about his experience in The Battle of the Bulge. He had a brother who was a glider pilot who died on his first run. Being able to talk about our military experiences has given us a unique bond.

I had a few colleges from which to choose, from all parts of the country. I chose to stay close to home (within an hour). I went to college right away. I was able to bring my engineering skills from the Marines to the classroom, as well as the maturity that other students didn't have. After college, I worked for some construction companies and realized I wanted to start my own company, which my wife encouraged me to do. We are growing steadily.

As the owner of a company, I do try to hire vets when they have the right experience. I wish I could say every one of them was great; some guys are still a bit lost. However, there is one employee who I think personifies the best of veterans. He is a Marine and is a tremendous asset to the company. He was without a home or job and was living in his car. When he couldn't make the payments, he lost the car. He walked to work 45 minutes each way. Sometimes a coworker would give him a ride home. He is never late, is respectful, gets along well with everyone and always asks for more responsibility. With the help of Veterans Outreach Center, he was able to return to the life he deserves.

I stay in touch my fellow vets; there is a strong connection between us, and six of us were together for most of my tour. If I were to offer one suggestion to civilians on talking to a veteran, especially one who has seen combat, it would be "Don't be afraid to listen. Don't shy away from that vet because he has a tough story to tell. Your listening helps his healing."

Jake

In high school, I wasn't sure what I wanted to do with my life, and a recruiter came to my high school. I had been hearing about terrorist attacks, Afghanistan and Iraq. Fighting them seemed like a noble thing to do, although I think back then I probably didn't use "noble" as my word. Probably more like something that just seemed like the right thing to do.

To join the Marines, I had to wait until I was 18. Like a lot of my guys my age, I was anxious to get going. Also, I didn't like the jobs they were offering to me based on my test scores. In other tests, I did well. The Air Force was interested in me, and they were offering me an opportunity in information management with a high security clearance. In 2005, when I turned 18, I was in the Air Force eight days after my birthday. I was about as fresh as I could be. It was my first time away from my mom (my parents were separated), and there I was in Boot Camp at Lackland Airforce Base in Texas. I did pretty well and was on their honor role, which only about 11% of troops earn.

It was really different than what I expected. Certainly it was more of a challenge than what I anticipated. I didn't know what to expect on any given day and from one day to the next. It could be drills, immunizations or training, and then maybe more drills. It was depressing for me not having the reassurance of a routine. It seemed like there was a lot of hurry up and wait.

Something I did know for certain: I needed to do 55 pushups in two minutes and 65 sit ups in two minutes. We were all sleep deprived. We got up at 4 a.m. When we heard the horns, I think we all groaned because it meant another whole day ahead of us marching and carrying a pack. This was to condition us for real-life combat and situations we might face. I guess I knew it was to make us confident that we could do more than we thought we could. I think the drill instructor carved me into shape, one aching muscle at a time.

In Boot Camp, one of the guys died. He had a heart condition no one knew he had. This was the first guy my own age that died like that. We all felt it.

After Boot Camp, things changed. Hurricane Katrina hit, and it was one of the deadliest hurricanes our country had ever faced. I had always thought of the enemy as other countries. Katrina took the lives of people of all ages. We were sent there to help. I had never seen anything like it. Everything had been flooded and was completely ransacked. There was garbage everywhere. I remember taking a bus to the base, and I saw a metal stairwell leading up to nothing. We were assigned to clean up base houses, clear away fallen trees, and get rid of the rotting garbage to keep the rats away. Some people needed rescuing, so we went on search and find missions.

In December, people came to a local church. We gave families and their kids anything we could, from hygiene kits to clothes. We gave toys to the kids. To see their faces light up to have a new toy was amazing. My squad helped the community with cleanup. It was all very different from what we had expected when we enlisted. It's not always about pointing the finger and killing bad people, it's also about supporting our own people and helping them regain their lives. These were Americans who needed our help; they had lost everything, and we did come to serve. It was a good eye opener for me as to how fortunate I had been.

After almost three months in hurricane relief, I went to several doctors because I was not feeling well. I had a lot of pain, and I couldn't seem to shake it off. I learned I had a bulging herniated disc. MRI diagnosed me with spinal stenosis, a degenerative disc disease. I had to leave the service. I would never get better, and I was permanently disabled. I had to say goodbye to the military life that I had chosen for myself.

I was only 20 years old. I felt useless, and it seemed that my life was already over. I was in tons of pain from which there was no escape. No position gave me any break from it. I tried walking, sitting, standing and even crawling. Ibuprofen wasn't touching it. Hydrocodone helped lessen the pain so that I felt like my young self again. To continue to escape the pain, I took more and more pills. Then there were no more refills, so I spent every dollar from my part-time job to get more. When I ran out, there wasn't exactly a withdrawal, but I felt like I had been hit by a Mack truck. I couldn't eat or sleep, and I didn't even want to breathe.

Then things really crashed. I had to borrow money for my car payment and my phone. I couldn't afford rent, so I stayed with my mom. When she and I clashed, I decided to go stay with friends and come back to get my stuff from her house. Not having my key, I went through the bathroom window, just as I had done as a kid when I forgot my key. I didn't realize she was home. When I heard noises I was freaked out and hid behind a dresser. My mom didn't know the footsteps were mine, and so she called the cops. Maybe in a movie it would seem funny. There was nothing funny about it for either of us.

I was at a hotel when the cops picked me up and charged me with burglary (I was only trying to get my own stuff back). Fortunately for me, through VOC, I went to Vet Court and was charged with simple trespassing, with no record. I got more medical help and counseling, did a mandatory stay at a halfway house and volunteered to rake mulch at a cemetery (no heavy lifting because I can't do it).

I have done some volunteer work, including making furniture for people receiving assistance from the Department of Human Services. I volunteered at Hope Initiatives. Also, I do presentations at the Health Association and provide them with some knowledgeable research I do in my spare time on addiction and recovery. I try to do my best to spread information I come across that can hopefully benefit others that were/are in the same position I was/am in.

My goal now is to go into the medical field. I am taking classes in entrepreneurship, have a nice girlfriend, live in a safe place, and have clean clothes and a new part-time job. I appreciate my life. For me, with the help I have received and the faith people have placed in me, I see that it's important not to believe we are not good enough. My words to other vets who have stumbled… "Believe in yourself. Don't underestimate yourself; give yourself more credit."

I know everyone has one question. Yes, my mom and I are fine.

Lynette Loomis

Rodney

As a late teen and young adult, I was pretty self-indulged; I went to a few colleges to pursue journalism and lived a life of relative comfort. I wasn't really committed to establishing myself. Deep down, I knew I could do better for myself. I enlisted in the Navy and performed repair maintenance on aircraft jet helicopters. After more than three and a half years, they were offering early discharge, and I took the offer.

Clearly my expectations about the possibilities that awaited me after my military service were not realized. For one thing, I really had no family to come home to. It didn't seem to matter to them whether I stayed in the fight or not. Also, my friends had moved on with their own lives. I almost felt like I had lost ground even though military service is honorable.

The biggest surprise was that I had actually thought there would be job opportunities. I felt that my service record was ignored, not understood or unappreciated. It was not easy to be a civilian; it was cold. I jumped on any opportunity that was available.

When I reached out to some places, everything felt political or I was buried in paperwork, until I got to VOC. They sat down with me, listened to me, and I could be honest and never felt I had to mask or apologize for my feelings. I listened to other veterans, and I knew they understood where I was coming from. One of the staff, Adam, went above and beyond to help me. He helped me achieve focus and assured me that I had what it takes to get it done, to create a good life for myself.

I am now certified in welding. It's hard to get hired without experience. I continue to take computer clinic classes; they are free at VOC. I work at Wilmot Cancer Center, and talking to the patients is the best part of my day. I am not a medical person; I'm just a regular guy to whom they can open up. They trust me with their fears and feelings. I hold their confidences close to my heart.

I want to remain focused and diligent and do work that fulfills me. I will become a journalist.

All vet stories are not war stories. We signed up to be away from our families for a just cause and to take advantage of benefits and opportunities we believed would be open to us for a better future. A soldier should never have to feel guilty because he or she left family for a while. They left for a purpose.

My advice? Don't forget where you came from.

The only failure is to not take an opportunity presented to you. No one said it would be easy; certainly Boot Camp taught us all that. We don't run from a challenge. We hit it head on.

Nick

On 9/11, I was in the back room at Wegmans, where I worked, and an older guy told me things I thought were just crazy until my boss told us to drop what we were doing and go home. When I got home, my roommate showed me the footage of the planes hitting the towers. I was consumed from that point forward. I told my parents I felt I had to do something, to find a connection to right the injustice that had been done.

I joined the Marines because my two best friends were joining, and it seemed like an adventure we could share together. We were pretty naive because after we all joined, we never saw each other again.

It wasn't until I was deployed to Afghanistan that I felt that connection. My first deployment wasn't too bad as we were in a somewhat controlled area. The second deployment was much worse. The Taliban controlled the area, and we lost some brave men from my unit. It was a bit of a culture shock as I was operating in an environment steeped in violence. This is the way of life, and has been for a very long time, in this region.

In this situation, there was no place to go, and you have no choice but to keep going. You are stranded in the middle of nowhere. We lived in FOBs, which stands for "forward operating base." There is no sense of safety. You rely on yourself because there is no safety net of 1,000 or 2,000 troops. There are maybe 50 or 60 other guys trying to fulfill their mission and make it home alive. It is amazing what the human spirit can endure when it has to.

I could have deployed again; however, I did not want to re-enlist. For the time I had left, I was stationed in California and instructed in a school for four months. My only thought was to have my freedom again. When we enlist, we give up freedom in order to serve as an efficiently disciplined and structured team. It is the only way it can work.

As soon as I crossed the border into New York State, it became really clear to me how much I had changed. I was lonely. I isolated myself from all the relationships I had before I enlisted. I am sure they wondered what was wrong with me. I wasn't the Nick they knew. Even when I was with people, I really wasn't with them. I guess I was preoccupied with trying to figure what I was going to do and coming to terms that there was something wrong with me.

My parents noticed a change in me, and they knew something was wrong. Unfortunately, I found a way to bring myself calm and peace. It was not a healthy outlet for me as I began to rely on drugs. There is a very logical reason why people do drugs: they make you feel better. For people who suffer from mental health disorders, including PTSD, drugs eliminate the negative symptoms very quickly. Unfortunately, the drugs then become more of a problem than what they were being used to treat. I sat my mother down to say I had something serious to tell her. She tried to guess, but I think nothing really prepared her for me saying I had a major drug issue.

At first my parents did not grasp the severity of it. Like me, they were lost and didn't know what to do. After many attempts at treatment and other forms of therapy, I eventually declined to a point where I was living in my car. My mom and dad would bring groceries to me. I tried to stay with them a few times. Due to my drug use, it was not acceptable for me to stay there. My little brother was in the Navy at the time. One day he found me and said we were going to rehab; two hours later I was back at home. My mom will tell you it was one of the hardest things she ever had to do. She basically said, "Here are your car keys. I will always love you, but you cannot be around our family in the state that you are in."

I was homeless for two months until I was arrested for possession of a forged instrument. My wife at the time had the same drug issues as I did. We grabbed a check book and cashed a check. Clearly I was desperate. I didn't even try to hide anything. I had hit rock bottom.

I called my mother from jail to let her know where I had ended up. Maybe she knew this kind of a call was inevitable, given the path I was on. She did what savvy moms do: she googled resources and found Veterans Outreach Center. They agreed to see me and were able to direct me to Vet Court. Judge Marks agreed that treatment was more appropriate for me than jail. Although I begged to go back home, Judge Marks knew that residential placement with other vets and counseling had a much better chance of setting me on the course I was really meant to be on. She was right. At the time, I figured I would go along with all of it because I did not want to return to jail.

After returning to my parents' home, I continued to do well. I never had one infraction or sanctions, and I never missed a counseling appointment. However, there was still the issue of the felony to be dealt with. A felony conviction would have limited me from ever realizing my potential. By now, I had started to believe in myself and in my future. Judge Marks fought on my behalf for months. Eventually, she prevailed, and I left that courtroom with all the opportunities I could have to succeed.

After that felony was behind me, Vet Court was contacted by CBS. They needed a veteran to share his story with David Martin, who is a reporter who works for Katie Couric on the Evening News. I agreed, and talking about my experiences triggered something in me, this hunger for a purpose. I wanted to fight injustice, and it renewed my purpose to serve my country in a different capacity. Therefore, I agreed to speak at the National Association of Drug Court Professionals in regard to my experience in Veterans Court. I thought it would be a small audience and invited my dad to accompany me. I was stunned to see some 4,000 people for my debut as a public speaker!

I hadn't prepared remarks because I thought it would feel staged and not genuine. This made the event organizers very nervous. I wanted to speak my truth and from my heart. At first I was sort of in a trance. However, I ended up finding that I excelled at public speaking, and it became the beginning of a journey that would take me across the country, speaking to many different audiences. On behalf of veterans, I have spoken at the White House, to Congress and with Chris Matthews MSNBC, advocating for Vet Treatment Court.

I have been asked how to help veterans struggling with re-entry. My advice:

- Seek resources in addition to the VA because other organizations work differently than the VA. (Rochester has the oldest free-standing veterans' program in the country, and they are willing to share what they know with other communities.)

- If a veteran you know is involved in the criminal justice system because of drug addiction, seek Veterans Court, drug court and treatment.

- Recognize that it can take years before someone is ready to change. They don't get off a plane or a bus after their deployment and rush to seek help. They are not always aware they have issues.

- Thousands of veterans struggle, and many believe there's no hope for them. I believed I had made a sacrifice and had given up something permanently and would suffer the rest of my life. With help, we can all find some type of peace. I have.

Cathy, Nick's Mom

Our son, Nick, returned from four years in the infantry in the Marines. He felt compelled to join after 9/11 at the age of 19. He was deployed to Afghanistan twice.

Nick returned home with PTSD. We were not equipped or qualified to help him. Our family was in crisis for several years and nothing we tried, or Nick tried, seemed to "stick." It was after a significant crisis that in our most desperate time, we, as Nick's parents, contacted Veterans Outreach Center with a plea for help. From the very first phone call, we were assured that VOC would do everything they could to assist Nick. It was a ray of hope we needed, and I really felt they were on our side.

There were some pretty extreme circumstances that VOC guided us through with their recommendations. When Nick first entered the criminal justice system, their advice of "leave him there" was critical, although it was hard for a mother to hear. VOC helped lead Nick through Veterans Court, where he first encountered Judge Marks.

We cannot adequately express our gratitude for VOC and the compassion, responsiveness and stability they provided to our family in this time of crisis. No matter how many times we called, sometimes with a concern and sometimes in a panic, a calming voice responded. The message was "We've got him." I felt our shoulders relax for the first time in a couple of years.

I think the thing that many parents don't realize is that VOC helps veterans and their spouses, parents… the entire family. Loving our sons and daughters does not qualify us to help them deal with the trauma of war.

Not all young men and women are compelled to serve in our military, but our country *depends* on them to volunteer to serve. They serve for all of us. They go in our place and, therefore, we are indebted to them.

The staff and volunteers of VOC and Judge Marks had to use their imagination to see past how Nick presented when they first met him to the inner soul, compassion and intelligence of our son. We believe that all of our veterans are worth saving, and many of them need support.

It was through the help of VOC that Nick was truly able to return. We will always remember the moment we saw Nick looking out at us through the window of Richards House. We knew for the first time since he joined the Marines that he was home.

Gary

At age 45, I realize that I have had undiagnosed mental health issues for decades. I had friends in high school, and things seemed OK for me, but I lacked a sense of direction for what I wanted to do with my life. With the encouragement of my uncle, a Navy veteran, I enlisted and spent my 19th birthday in the Navy. Submarines were my goal.

When you are on a sub for numerous sea trials, things you thought you could manage become bigger than life. One guy bullied me a lot, probably because I was never very good at forming relationships with a lot of people. It was like they knew some code I was not privy to. I became pretty anxious and had that pit in my stomach all the time. There was no point in complaining, of course. I was in the Navy, not a whiner, and I knew things would just get worse for me. I think this guy thought I was a bagger and wanted to shirk my duty. That was not the case; I was trying to stay out of his way, and I didn't want to get in a fight with him. The guy was like the devil and seemed to take great pleasure in making me miserable.

In high school, I had friends who were all different from one another. One was a jock, another a brain, one a class clown, and another smoked cigarettes. We were all friends. I was not used to the bullying thing. In fact, if I had seen someone being bullied, I would have stepped in. On the submarine, I did not fit in.

When we were on liberty in Canada, I got pretty drunk. They sent me to a counselor to talk about my "alcoholism," which seemed odd to me. I didn't think one night's drunkenness made me an alcoholic. (My father had been an alcoholic, and I had a good sense of what that behavior was like. It didn't seem like me.) Looking back, maybe that was the reason they could use to get me evaluated. I needed some help and advice. When you are way down underwater, there is really no one to turn to.

I felt confused and disorientated. Had I understood mental health issues, I might have realized that medication would have helped me, and I could have stuck it out. They gave me an honorable discharge. I went back to Rochester and stayed at my parents' home. Next, a friend took me with him to New Hampshire. I got a job as a cook because I cooked on the submarine. I do make a mean chicken teriyaki.

For more than 20 years, I went from job to job, some 50 or so jobs, and moved around a lot. I've made poor decision after poor decision, looking for something I could not find and could not explain. I lived in shelters in several states. After a surgery, I got behind in my rent and collected welfare. I came back to Rochester and stayed at Richards House with other vets as part of the Homeless Veterans' Reintegration Program (HVRP). Felix, the cat, used to crawl into the window at night and sleep with me. Felix was great company. Unfortunately for me, my roommate didn't like having a cat in the room.

I got counseling, participated in art therapy, and was in a safe, structured place where I did not feel judged, even though I am an atheist. For my chemical imbalance, I got on the medications I should have been on years ago. I take several meds. In fact, I realize I must have been worse than I thought.

VOC helped me find my own place through Supportive Services for Veteran Families (SSVF). They provide supportive services to very low-income vets who want to transition into permanent housing. They even helped me set up housekeeping! The training I received helped me get a job so I can take care of myself. Everybody at VOC has helped me extremely well in many ways!

My life could have been different. I should have been less prideful and sought help much sooner. My chemical imbalance has cost me many relationships. Counseling and the right meds have helped me enormously. My outlook on life is much more positive now. When other vets ask me about my journey, I tell them not to be afraid to be who you need to be, who you are in your heart. Accept the help that is offered to you. It can open up a new world for you.

Matt and His Kids

My kids were older than some kids of active troops. My son was 18 years old, and my daughter was 8. They were used to dad being gone, as the Coast Guard required much of that while I was active duty (eight years). Additionally, the fears of safety and worry were somewhat common, as I was also a Police Officer with the Rochester City Police Department.

After I was recalled by the Coast Guard (Department of Homeland Security) in support of both Operation Enduring Freedom and Operation Iraqi Freedom, the kids had to say goodbye. I was deployed to conduct antiterrorism missions at the Port of Miami AOR. I was ramped up to go to the Middle East (Port of Bahrain), but, fortunately, I was given orders to Officer Candidate School and did not have to deploy to the Middle East. While I was on recall, I was stationed at the Tactical Law Enforcement Team South (U.S. Coast Guard Air Station Opa Locka).

I trained every day with Petty Officer Nathan Bruckenthal. He and two U.S. Navy sailors were killed while intercepting a waterborne suicide attack on the Khor Al Amaya Oil Terminal off the coast of Iraq in the northern Persian Gulf. This impacted me greatly. I became somewhat withdrawn, as someone I personally knew, had broken bread with, laughed with, and played hard with, had been killed.

The calls home to my kids actually made me feel better. I didn't forget that there was a bigger picture, and it wasn't about me; that would be selfish. My kids told me that they were actually proud of what I was doing. I was making a difference; I was protecting the people of the United States. They were sad I was gone, yes. They also were proud and happy that I was committed to making the "world safer by the work I was doing."

I am one of only a few who would say the recall was a positive event. I was actually struggling with some issues because of losing my father and a best friend with whom I had gone through the police academy, both within less than a year. I was not sheltered from sadness or anger. However, the recall assignment helped me to refocus and get back on track. My kids and wife saw the difference. After some time, they "liked again who I was turning back into." I am thankful that I was able to serve, grow *and* maintain my family.

Amy, Military Wife of a Solider with Multiple Deployments

I have talked with a lot with other military wives. There are some common themes for our husbands, who have been deployed a number of times.

- Some of them have gone through absolute hell. Their dealing with it is like a seven-layer dip. They deal with one aspect of it, and then they dig down to deal with the next layer.

- No matter how much we love them, we can't fix their pain. It is a process and not necessarily a short one. Their issues might not pop up for years. Then something will trigger a very strong emotion, and we all think, "Where did that come from?"

- They fought for their country, and sometimes what keeps them alive and going is the thought of coming home. Coming home might be idealized, and when the reality doesn't fit their dream, it can be emotionally devastating.

- It's hard for them to talk to people who really don't listen or to those who may not even appear to care. It is isolating when their lifelong friends want them to "get over it" when they have no sense of what "it" is.

- In the military, there were standards, and they had to meet them. There was absolute accountability. When they run up against a contractor who does shoddy work, doesn't show up and never finishes the job, it makes them nuts. If they had not done their job, people would be dead.

- Panic and anxiety attacks are unpredictable, so the vet may shy away from social contact so he doesn't embarrass himself or his family.

- Making sure their home is safe is very important to them. They may "check the perimeter" a few times a night to make sure everything is as it should be. Even though they are not on a mission, it's a habit that affected lives when they were deployed.

- For some guys, going into battle was easier than talking about their feelings.

- Listening matters. Don't finish their sentences or project your feelings onto them. Be patient. They are all heroes and deserve our love, patience and respect.

PART TWO

Hans

Lynette Loomis

Me as a Pup

I remember a little bit about being a young pup. There was a bunch of us, and it was hard to get my share of my mother's milk. I had to climb over my brothers and sisters, just like they climbed over me. We were all black, and when we nursed, I think it was hard for the humans to tell where one puppy began and the other one ended. However, if one of us pooped, it was pretty easy to tell which end was which.

We might have looked a lot alike, but we could tell who was who by the way we smelled. All puppies smell great, and we each had our own smell, as did our mom. It's pretty clear that dogs have better noses than humans do because humans seem to call each other by name rather than just giving each other a good sniff.

One time, we all went for a ride. None of us had been in a car before, and my brother threw up stuff. He ate it again right away, so I guess he felt better. We went to a place called a vet (short for "veterinarian," which is too long a word for me anyway). They were nice people except when it came time to get a shot, which is a little pointy thing that stings for a minute. Then we each got a treat, and I forgot about the shot. I love TREATS. I am not sure why I only seem to get one TREAT at a time when I could eat lots more.

As we got bigger, people came to pet us and look at us. The family my mom and we lived with said they had to give us all away because there would not be enough food for all of us. This was confusing to me because it seemed like the stuff they threw in the garbage can after every meal would have filled our stomachs just fine.

One day, many people came to see my brothers and sisters and me. A girl put me in a box with a blanket and took me home with her. She seemed nice, but I think maybe I was a little more work than she expected. When I was with my mom, she licked me to make me go poop and pee and then cleaned me up. The girl didn't seem to know she was supposed to do this. She used her angry voice when I peed in the house. (She went out in the morning and didn't come home till later.) There was also a thing with one of her shoes…

The girl put me back in the box. I thought maybe we were going for a ride or back to see my brothers and sisters or maybe to play with other puppies. I was surprised that we went to a big building where there was a lot of barking. I didn't recognize a single smell. I heard the girl saying, "I tried to find him a home. No one wants a dog right now. I just can't take care of him." I decided I wanted to go home. The girl drove away and left me there.

I didn't know what a kill shelter was, but the man looked sad, and that worried me. Maybe this wasn't a good place after all. They put me in a cage, and I didn't have a lot of room and certainly no place to run around. It was scary for me. The man with the deep, smooth voice said, "Don't you worry, little guy, someone will want a beautiful dog like you. There is a family out there somewhere just waiting for you." Turns out, he was right.

On the Road Again

One day, after I had been in the shelter a while, a lady came to get me. She said she was from Rudy's Rescue. They recued dogs and found them homes. I did not know what "rescue" meant, and no one had ever called me Rudy. Clearly, I was confused. The nice man seemed very pleased that I was leaving. I tried to be pleased, too, and wagged my tail.

The lady told me that we would drive for two hours and then someone else would drive me some more. (Since I have gotten older, I have heard humans say that some people live in their cars. I think this is what they meant. I lived in a car for days and got to go out for walks and stuff.) I was glad I was in some of the cars because sometimes there were old French fries and stuff I could reach with my tongue. It made the ride more fun. The drivers all talked to me, and sometimes they turned on a radio and howled with the music, so I howled too.

When I finally got to a house, I was pretty tired of cars. I had my own soft bed and new toys. I thought maybe this was just another stop along the way. Or was it going to be my new home? Then I was told they would find me a good home. WHAT? Wasn't THIS my new home? It appears I was at a temporary home they call a foster home. I met a Les and Jocelyn, who were really nice. They talked with someone they referred to as the "head pooper scooper."

This head pooper scooper (her real name was Amy) was pretty fussy. I knew some people liked me a lot. Amy thought they were not the right family for me. Amy had a parrot that was pretty talkative and was always telling me to sit, stand or stay. I had never heard or seen a talking bird and wondered if all birds were that bossy. I decided that if any bird ever expected me to chirp, I was putting my paw down.

Amy introduced me to Tom, who seemed to know a lot about dogs like me. Amy and Tom would always say what a great puppy I was. This made me very proud. Amy and Tom promised me my next stop would be my last, and my new family would love me forever. Amy said she saw something in my eyes and knew I could help veterans in need. They said I had what it took to reach the souls of guys who felt they had been forgotten. We looked into each other's eyes a lot. Her husband had been a Marine, and when she got one phone call, she sounded excited. "A home for veterans? He'd be perfect!"

Before I went to the home for veterans, I had to be "socialized." I thought I was pretty social already. I gave everybody I met a nice welcome sniff. What more was there? I went to stay with Tom and his wife, Jody. Amy still helped me with learning new things in her puppy class. That was fun because, when I got it right, I got TREATS.

There were some interesting looking and great smelling things Amy said NO dog should ever have, even if we begged or did neat tricks (or ate them off the counter), like chocolate. I have heard that people beg for chocolate, especially when they're dieting. I really don't understand all of that.

I knew Amy loved me a lot because she was also pretty fussy about what I ate. I am not fussy at all and even eat stuff that isn't food. In fact, leather boots are pretty tasty. She asked me to tell you all about this so you can take good care of your dogs, too. (See Appendix One)

Amy says to look for USDA Certified Organic ingredients, which is pretty confusing to me because I can't read. She says to look for the round, green USDA Organic label on foods. USDA (who would name anybody Usda?) Organic means no synthetic fertilizers, pesticides or genetically modified organisms. I probably wouldn't like anything I can't say in dog talk. I like simple sounding stuff like meat, beans, carrots and TREATS. And no fancy stuff that has a whole bunch of ingredients—just the basics. I can't count up to seven, but Amy says even my snacks (like peanut butter, cheese, applesauce, yogurt, roasted nuts, seeds and pretzels) should have seven or fewer recognizable items. This science stuff wears me out, so I just close my eyes.

I love cookies, and Amy made me some that were great. (The recipe is at the end of the book.) I could have eaten them all at once. Amy said, "No, Hans. Some of these have to go in the freezer, or they will spoil." We could have avoided the whole freezer thing if she had just put that cookie sheet a little closer to me…

Lynette Loomis

Take Me for a Ride in the Car...or Truck

Tom picked me up and took me to his house. His wife, Jody, was nice. His big dog, Max, was scary to me at first. Eventually, we became buddies. Of course, we always had to test out who was strongest and wrestled a lot over toys, a ball or a rawhide bone. I was no match for Max when it came to tug of war. After a while, we just lay down next to each other and took a nap. Tom said it looked like we were hugging each other, which is silly because we all know dogs don't hug. Right?

Tom, Max and I loved to go in the truck together. That high truck seat was tough for me at first, but Max showed me how to do it. I am a smart dog and caught on right away. When Tom got out of the truck, there were always neat toys to chew on like his sunglasses, cell phone charger, rear window defroster wiring or an interior door handle. They weren't very tough; I usually had them chewed up in minutes.

I thought I should let Tom know I was grown up. When he tried to get back in the truck, I wouldn't move over. He would agree that the driver's seat really belonged to me and would put the leash on me and let me leave through the driver's door. Then he would open up the rear door and let me climb into the back seat. I loved this game because I always won.

I took a few more trips to the vet when I lived with Tom and Jody. I noticed that Max had pills and I didn't have any, which was not fair at all because I was a good dog, too. I climbed up onto their kitchen counter top and grabbed a bunch of pills. Each one was wrapped separately, and I had to be very patient and open each one by itself (and I have never liked the taste of foil anyway). Rather than be impressed with my puppy finesse, Jody made Tom call some poison place for dogs. They put something called hydrogen peroxide down my throat, which isn't as much fun as it sounds. Barfing everything back up wasn't much fun either.

Tom must have really liked driving to the emergency vet place because we went there another time, too. I think he would really rather have finished watching the Notre Dame/USC game one Saturday night. They call Tom's basement a "man cave." It doesn't look much like a cave to me. (I watch National Geographic, and I know these things.) There is no rock on the walls or dirt on the floor. There is plenty of what Jody calls Notre Dame Gold with Kelly Green Trim. I am more of a brown guy myself. Off we went again, and this time I didn't have to barf anything up but was given pills (pills in cheese go down really easy). That night, they let me sleep in their bed so I could protect them from moths and stuff. I slept with them every night after that.

People are pretty strange about the whole pee and poop thing. They seem to go inside the house in a little room with a big bowl of water in it; I had to go outside. When I had to go, I would sit at the kitchen door leading to the garage to let Tom know I had to go outside. My favorite time was 4 a.m. Tom didn't dress up too much for this and wore boxer shorts. I had never seen a boxer in shorts. I had seen dogs in sweaters. This term was very odd to me. Also, there were no pictures of boxers on his shorts that I could see; I was really confused. He also wore a t-shirt and bare feet (the only way to walk from my point of view). He would say, "Go break," and I would pee, and then we would go back to bed for a while. There is some confusion for me on "Take a break" and "Go break," but I am figuring it out.

Near Christmastime, Tom thought he could leave the house without me. Max might have been fine with being left behind. Not me. I decided to explore all the neat stuff Jody had left out. I rearranged all the pine cones, took the beard off the Irish Santa, and ate the candy out of the dish (it was probably meant for me anyway). I tried to bury all the little snowmen throughout the house so Max and I could find them again. The knocked-over coffee table was an accident. When Tom got home, his face showed me he didn't think my game had been my best idea. He cleaned it all up before Jody got home, and I just went to sleep. All that rearranging was exhausting.

We went to a big grocery store, Wegmans, where I could meet the people who helped me come to my new home. It had the best smells all in one place that I had ever smelled. I was allowed to go there because I was a service dog in training. I am not sure who I was serving as they seemed to have lots of people there to help their customers without me cleaning off bones or licking the floor. I got petted and talked to and, of course, was given TREATS. I love TREATS (or did I already mention that?)!

Lynette Loomis

Partying and Sports Bars

I also was friends with Brian. He and I did all sorts of fun things. We went to birthday parties with lots of kids, and they all wanted to pet me. They had a lot of sticky stuff on their fingers that tasted good. I learned about birthday present tape, which was really hard to get off my paws. I would try to hold onto it with one paw, and then it would get stuck on the other. Then I would start all over again. Brian laughed and got rid of that pesky tape for me.

A kangaroo? Me like a kangaroo? I have seen them on television, and I don't think I am anything like them, with their little short front legs. Brian says I am like a kangaroo because I can jump very high. The kitchen couther isn't really *that* high, and when food was left there, I assumed it was for me. I have learned that really isn't true, but I am a lot smarter now that I am a big dog.

The first day I was with Mary and Brian, I sat in Mary's lap, and we watched some TV. Then Brian turned off the TV and went up the stairs. I followed right along and hopped up onto their bed. (That's what the dogs on TV do, and I am a smart dog.) I got next to Mary, gave her a little lick on the cheek and put my head on her shoulder. This sleeping with people is the best.

One afternoon, Brian said we were going to a sports bar. There weren't any balls or Frisbees for me to catch. I thought maybe we were in the wrong place. When we first went inside, the guys at the bar didn't pay too much attention to me. They thought I was a service dog, I guess. I think most humans need a service dog because it's pretty clear to me that we dogs see, smell and hear better than humans do. And they could use the help; they miss a lot.

When Brian told the guys at the bar I was going to live with veterans and why, everything changed. The guys got off their stools and came over to pet me. Brian said it was lucky I didn't have a bald spot on my head from all that petting, but I'm pretty tough. One of the men was German, and he said my name meant "gift from God." I think I

47

was the one getting all the gifts. The cook brought me out a boneless chicken all to myself! The guys told me about their military experiences or that of their brothers or sisters. Even people in the dining room came into the bar area to see me. It was such great fun I forgot to be disappointed that they didn't have any balls to catch or fetch. I have been there a few more times. Brian says they treat me like royalty. I think their treat me like their friend.

Brian and I also went to a nursing home, which isn't really where nurses live. It's where older people live who need some help. A lot of these people used to have dogs, and they like to pet me. The nurses keep TREATS for me. I have to make sure I stay out of the way of the wheels on the chairs and don't get my toes or tail pinched. Some of the people don't use words. I think I understand what they are saying by the way they pet me. I think their hands are saying, "Nice dog." Sometimes when they pat my head, they seem to calm down, maybe remembering their own dogs and a time when things were easier or less painful. I love these visits, and when we go there now, I know exactly which way to turn off the elevator, even when the humans don't know where they are.

When Brian thought I was ready, he brought me to my new home and introduced me to the guys. There were a lot of them of all ages, colors, sizes and smells. Everyone in my new family of brothers was a veteran. Like me, they all needed a home, a place to be accepted and a place to start over. I am going to tell you about "that other animal" and about a few of the guys.

After All, I'm Still a Puppy

Adult people think kids and puppies are just smaller versions of their parents. We're not. We're more fun. We know how to amuse ourselves. Like the time I was by myself in the living room. The arms of that leather sofa were calling, "Hans, Hans." Being the good dog that I am, I went over for a look, a quick a sniff, then a lick. This changed to a small nibble to check for color and texture, next a small chew to see if it would taste good; it did. I decided to throw myself into it with all my heart. Those sofa arms were great, and the leather cushions were just as tasty. The sofa now has a blanket on it where there used to be leather. My naps are undisturbed.

I like to go hunting. I don't carry a gun of course. Dogs don't need guns to hunt because we are pretty quick on our feet, and humans wear all that stuff to make them look like trees and leaves. Really? Any self-respecting animal can smell humans a long way off, and my wolf cousins can smell prey more than a mile away and can hear things miles away. Humans are not as sneaky as they think they are and seem to like their hunting outfits a lot. We really don't seem to shoot at anything, but it's great to walk in the woods.

The Groomer

My kind, black labs, have been bounding into the water to haul nets and fetch ropes from the ocean forever. And labs also retrieve game in fields and forests, and don't eat it unless we are told we can. (Please don't confuse my kind with those golden retrievers, who are very nice. They are not labs.)

My ancestors did just fine without being taken to a groomer. (Are they laughing at me now?) One day, we went to the groomer. The place smelled like lots of dogs, which are smells I really like. Of course, somehow I was expected to sit and stand on a table when I had spent months and months being trained NOT to stand on tables. If they wonder why dogs are hard to train…

Up I went. They wanted to brush me. I wasn't sure about this brushing as the guys at the house don't have much hair, which saves them a lot of time. I get brushed at home a lot because they say I shed enough every day to stuff a pillow. This groomer brushing is much more intense. I put up with it. Then they look in my ears and take a little cotton ball and check my ears. I can hear perfectly fine, and putting a cotton ball in my ear does not make me hear any better. What are they thinking?

They also cut my nails. This is a leap of faith for me. I have chewed an emery board from time to time, and I really think walking on the sidewalk everyday has the same feel to it. They use this noisy buzzing little grinder thing that sounds like the most irritating mosquito ever. I put up with it.

They've tried to brush my teeth. Again, this is confusing because I know I am NOT supposed to have brushes in my mouth, and here they go and try to put one in it. I tried to spit it out. They put it back in. It did have some tasty stuff on it.

I put up with it all. Why? Because I hoped that I would get a TREAT, and I did. Not as good as some, but I am pretty easy going and would not want to hurt anyone's feelings by rejecting a TREAT.

Felix the Cat

When I came home to the house with all the guys, I could tell they were worried about me. This made no sense. A lot of the guys petted me and played with me. I had cool toys, and some of them made great noises. I had lots of water and was fed twice a day in a bowl I didn't have to share with anybody. There were TREATS when I did something they wanted me to do. Life seemed perfect.

And then I saw HIM. The CAT. The cat was the same color as me. However, he wasn't like me at all. He didn't bark; he made a hissing sound whenever he saw me. He was smaller than me and had smaller claws. They looked pointier than mine, sharper maybe. I think I could have squashed him if I sat on him or shook him like one of my toys, but the guys never let me get that close. They carried me around whenever the cat and I were in the same room.

"You don't want to mess with Felix, little Hans. He's 15 years old and is pretty street smart, especially when it comes to dogs. Those claws will scratch your nose so bad you'll be whining for weeks." I never thought of myself as much of a whiner, more of a barker.

I thought about the only other time I had met a cat. It wasn't pretty. He was a little guy about the size of small slipper (I had lots of experiences with slippers and know my sizes). I tried to play with him. I pounced toward him to signal that I wanted to play chase. He must not have understood dog talk. He arched his back. It seemed like his fur went straight up in the air, which was a pretty weird thing to look at because it puffed him up to be the size of two slippers. This weird little hiss came out of his mouth as if he were one of those lions we see on TV. I thought it was pretty funny…until he swiped at my nose. That was the end of play time. I guess now I know cat speak. When the back arches and this hiss comes out, back away.

When I went to get on Patrick's bed, he and I being buddies and all, the cat was there. I had a choice. It could be a showdown like on TV with a lot of barking and hissing, or I could "be the bigger dog." There were other guys who needed a buddy like me to help them fall asleep, and I decided I would move onto another bed.

I am not sure why Felix didn't like me when we never even got a chance to play. It could be because they found him under a porch, cold and hungry, when he was little. We were both orphans until we got to live with the guys. Maybe he was afraid that there wasn't room for the two of us in the house, and he would end up under a porch again. I think I understand that, no matter what color our fur is, we all want to belong somewhere.

Lynette Loomis

Glen

A lot of my guys tell me about the dogs they had when they were kids, like Glen and Princess. She was a family dog, in a much smaller family than mine, of course. She followed the kids all around and played with them every day. She even protected them if she thought they were in trouble. We dogs do that a lot. We even will let kids feed us the stuff from the table they don't want, like green beans. Squash is a little harder to sneak, but if it splats on the floor and we lick it up in a hurry, usually the parents can't tell. Then everyone is happy.

If Glen was having a bad day or messed up at school, he knew Princess loved him no matter what. I know he loved her a lot because when he told me Princess passed away while he was in the service, his eyes got teary. He said they buried her in the country with lots of land around her and trees and birds and squirrels. That sounded like a good place to me, and I am sure she was content.

Sometimes the guys tell me stuff I don't think they really tell each other. "I love my country; my whole family is patriotic," Glen said. "I'm a simple guy. I wanted to serve my country as a Marine, come home, get in the right company and raise a family. Hans, let me tell you, it hasn't been that easy. It hasn't been easy at all.

"I was a firefighter and a first responder. There was a plane that was flying over us too close, and we could hear the radio chatter telling them to pull back. We got ready for the worst. And it was the worst. We heard the crash and saw a mushroom cloud, and the sirens went off as we raced to the plane.

"We lost 11 soldiers and kept three alive. Some of them were my friends. Even those I didn't know, I cared about. After that day and every day still, I wonder if there was something else, something more, I could have done that would have let one more son return home. Hans, my guilt was so great I retreated from the world, and it seemed to get harder, not easier. I still have trouble getting out of my own head.

"I bounced around a lot after the service. I parked cars, did odd jobs and sorted mail. I went to college. I lived in a men's shelter for a while. I just couldn't find myself, and I got more and more depressed.

"You know what buddy? Being with you feels like being with Princess again. No matter what I tell you, you listen. You seem to sense my moods even when I don't feel like talking. You know when to back off and when to come close. Rubbing your head or your stomach calms me. You make me feel needed again. You're a good boy, Hans."

I think Glen is a good boy too.

Patrick

The good thing about being a dog is that we don't expect too much. I never heard of a PhD in dog. Personally, I don't want to be on TV prancing around on a leash in front of a lot of people. I am much more of a bounder than a prancer. If I can get from here to there, how high my tail is seems a little silly to me. I try not to judge. We all do what we need to do for a TREAT.

Patrick walks me a lot. We go out before the sun is up and while everyone else is still asleep. I like this time of day. I can focus on all the great smells on the sidewalk and in the grass. Sometimes there is even a hamburger wrapper I can chew. Patrick calls that litter, like it's a bad thing. I really think people leave stuff on the sidewalk just for us dogs. I appreciate that. If Patrick would let me, I would scarf down all that stuff, and there would be no litter at all.

I know when we are going for a walk because he reaches for his jacket and my leash. That way, I can pull him around the block in case he's still tired. He says our walks clear his head. I am pretty sure he likes me better than that cat because he doesn't take him for any walks. Sometimes we both sleep on his bed; that took a while. Maybe it goes to show that anybody can get along if they try hard enough, although the occasional cat TREAT under the beds helped. Maybe some people just aren't getting enough TREATS.

I don't really have many bad days. If I mess up and feel bad, I just take a nap and start over. It doesn't seem to be that way with people. They can hold onto a hurt like I hold tight to a bone. The only reason I let go of a bone is if I see something even better. I guess it's like that with the guys. They hold onto their bad stuff until they can find their way to something better. And I understand about trying the same bad thing more than once. I keep thinking some great smelling stuff will be really tasty. It always gives me a stomach ache, but then I go and do it again.

I think Patrick is like that, too. He was a mechanic in the service. After he got out, he said he felt lost and started to drink and do something called crack. He kept trying it. It really didn't make him feel any better. Just like me, he had no home until he came here.

He says he's on the road to recovery now. He seems pretty positive to me because he is always telling me that I am a smart dog. When I mess up, he doesn't yell. He just finds something else for me to do. (I have heard them say it is called redirecting; I am not too sure about all that.) He never makes me feel bad about myself, and my tail is always up when I am with him. I think everyone should always feel like they can hold their tail up and have another chance.

When he leaves our house and gets his own place, I know we will miss each other. He can come back and visit and maybe take me for a walk. After he gets a job, he told me he is going to volunteer to help animals who stay at a shelter. He will be good for them, and I think they will be good for him, too.

Daniel

I am not a very good counter, but 285 Army combat missions seems like it must be a lot. Daniel told me that his job was to "take out valued assets." I am not sure what that is all about. I think it means that he had to get rid of the people who could hurt the rest of us. He told me sometimes they would do two missions a day in Iraq.

He was only 18 when he went over there, which is a very long time in dog years and pretty young in human years. He and the other guys would track where their enemies were day by day in a hostile environment. I think this must be like being around a pack of wolves that don't want you in their territory and will tear you apart with their teeth, except people use guns and bombs. Either way, it is very scary because you never know from minute to minute if you will live to see the sun shine again, or if you will be so hurt you can't walk.

One day when we were resting on the sofa, the one I chewed the arms off that were really tasty, he told me about being shot at. He said that there were armed bodyguards at the entrance of every place the enemy leaders were, ready to shoot him and his buddies. They took machine gun fire, and they gave it back. "It's not like in a lot of war movies, where everyone is fearless, Hans. It's really scary, except that when you're in the middle of it, you aren't scared. You do what you were trained to do, to protect your squad and complete the mission. When it's over, you might get the shakes and want to throw up. Then you go out and do it again.

"When I came home on leave, it all caught up with me. I was dead to the world, and I had no feeling. How do you even talk about this stuff to someone who has nothing like it in their life? One night, I had a flashback about being shot at and drove into a wall. I really hurt my knee. I had two surgeries, and that ended my military career because I couldn't go back to the infantry. That's about all I knew how to do other than a metal trade certificate I picked up in high school.

"I bounced around a lot. My parents were both gone. I stayed with my grandparents, then some friends. No place was home. I self-medicated to try to deal with my feelings and fears, which means drugs. Twice I went into rehab. I wouldn't let it work for me."

Daniel and I have fun together. I can kind of tell when he is feeling low and try to lift him up. He says I keep him in the present. When he's happy, I might give him a nip in the butt to play with him, and he laughs. He tells me about the dogs he had growing up, a pit bull and a golden-lab. He is very patient with me. As a puppy, of course all I want to do is play, but he knows I have to sit and heel. When I get it right, I can play with my squeaky toys or get a Milk Bone. (There is no such thing in my mind as too many TREATS. Miss Judy says they don't need a fat lab that can't get up the stairs. I am still thinking about that one.)

Daniel loves his motors. He likes to Jet Ski and does a motocross thing and rides snow mobiles. When he leaves us, he wants to own his own business and build custom motorcycles. Maybe he could build a sidecar, and I could ride with him and have my own goggles. Of course, he wants a dog. I think everybody should have a dog. He says he and I are just starting out and starting over. I know we are both going to be OK.

Andy

Andy says that dogs love him more than the ladies do. I don't know about that. He and I were buddies from the first day we met. He told me his mom used to rescue dogs all the time, and I know I would like her, too.

He told me he started out life on a pretty good path. He was president of his class in high school, an All Star athlete, and coached kids in sports. He and his dad built a log cabin in the woods, and there was a special place for their dogs. One time, there was a blizzard, and they couldn't reach the dogs for two days. He said that really scared him. When they finally got to the dogs, Andy said there was a lot of jumping around. I wasn't sure if it was Andy or the dogs that were doing the jumping. Maybe all of them.

He joined the Army for stability and college and the kind of training that would help him have a good life. In Desert Storm, he was in military intelligence. He must have been smart because you wouldn't put the runt of the litter for brains in a job like that, right? He broke his ankle pretty badly and got an early discharge. Then he knew there would be no scholarship for college sports.

When Andy talks to me about being a kid and swimming and camping with his dogs, I know he misses them. His eyes look sad when he talks about his son, whom he hasn't seen in a while. "I took the wrong path more than once and did some pretty bad stuff, Hans. I took things that weren't mine and turned myself in. I had hit rock bottom. Be glad that dogs don't do drugs, Hans, because they really mess you up. I went to Vet Court and stayed in a place (VOC) where I could start over. When they told me I was going to live with 25 guys, I thought it was a joke and that it would never work."

I could have told him that 25 guys is the perfect number, but I think he had to find that out for himself. He and I wrestle on the floor, and we never hurt each other. We go for a lot of walks. Andy wants us to get a pass for a dog park, which I think is a place just for dogs where we don't have to be on a leash and can go swimming and sniff each other. That sounds like fun to me.

I know from going on walks there are a lot of different paths we can take. Some are not very nice and even scary. Other paths take us to a great place. I hope when Andy leaves us, his next path is the right one for him.

Shane

Shane was in the Navy and on a ship. I have never been on a ship. It sounds like a big place with no grass to run on. He told me that when he was a boy he had a cocker spaniel named Lady. She would wake him up in the morning and lick his face. I think dogs are better than washcloths when it comes to washing faces. We don't miss anything.

"Hans, I am an addict, and I can never go back to that life. If I wasn't living here now, I'd be dead. I was homeless, had no place to go, wasn't eating, and drinking whenever I could. I was a mess." He told me he had tried some programs and never really let them work for him. Now he is a sponsor and helps other people.

Sometimes Shane and I don't need words. If he is stressed, he smells different and his body is tense. I know that it's time for us to play or walk off our energy. He says that with so many of the guys walking with me, I should wear something on my leg to show how many miles I walk in a day. I'm not sure why that's important. If my buddies need to walk, all they have to do is get my leash. That's what buddies do for each other.

As a dog, I don't have many dreams. I want some walks, some great naps, toys, the occasional squirrel to chase, and lots and lots of TREATS. I want to be loved and sleep with the guys and have my belly scratched. Shane has dreams. He wants to stay sober and go back to being a welder with a steady job. He wants to rescue a shelter dog and have a wife and kids. He says that with God's help and our house, he will make it. I believe he will.

My First Birthday

I love parties because parties mean TREATS! For my first birthday, the guys threw me a birthday party in the back. We don't really have a deck or a patio, but we do have a paved area with some picnic tables. We all wore pointy little party hats, even the toughest of the veterans. I think being with me lets these brave men feel that it's OK to be silly, to laugh from their belly up. They do it for me. I wore my hat for them. We all laughed in our own way, and then I got down to business. My present was a big rawhide bone.

Lynette Loomis

Epilogue

I Am Done Moving on Down the Road

My rambling days are behind me; this is my forever home. For my buddies, this is just a stop on their journey. You can't tell just by looking at them that their heart might be full of pain, guilt or worry. While each of them was proud to serve their country, it can be hard to return to civilian life. But we are here for each other, always.

Lynette Loomis

Appendix

Hans' and Amy's Cookies

INGREDIENTS:
- 2+ cups old-fashioned rolled oats
- 1 tbsp. baking powder
- 1 cup ground chicken
- 1 cup natural unsalted peanut butter
- 1/2 cup water or low-sodium chicken broth
- 3 tbsp. chopped fresh parsley
- 1 tbsp. chopped garlic

1. Preheat oven to 400°F. In a food processor, pulse oats and baking powder into a fine powder. Add chicken, peanut butter, water, parsley and garlic and pulse to combine. With a spatula, scrape mixture from food processor and form into ball.
2. Arrange ball between two sheets of parchment paper and roll out to 1/4-inch thick. Cut into 1-inch squares and arrange on a parchment-lined baking sheet.
3. Bake until golden, about 15 minutes. Cool completely. Store refrigerated in a sealed container.

No, Hans, No

Amy says these are things we should never have, even if we beg for them. – Hans

(These are <u>not</u> TREATS)

1. Chocolate
2. Raisins
3. Mouse and Rat Poisons (rodenticides)
4. Vitamins and Minerals (Vitamin D3, iron, etc.)
5. NSAIDs (ibuprofen, naproxen, etc.)
6. Cardiac Medications (calcium channel blockers, beta-blockers, etc.)
7. Cold and Allergy Medications (pseudoephedrine, phenylephrine, etc.)
8. Antidepressants (selective serotonin reuptake inhibitors)
9. Xylitol
10. Acetaminophen (e.g., Tylenol)
11. Caffeine Pills

The whole pill thing was confusing to me because I heard Amy say that, if people did not keep me busy, I could be a real pill. What?

Depression and Suicide

Many people are surprised when a friend or loved one attempts, or succeeds, in taking his or her life. The stressors of deployment are real. Prolonged exposure to life-threatening events, physical pain and major life changes contribute to depression and sometimes to thoughts of suicide.

- Listen with an open ear; don't dismiss or judge their thoughts and feelings.

- Be aware of behavioral changes, such as withdrawal from activities, friends or family, or loss of interest in activities they used to enjoy.

- Watch for use of drugs, both legal and illegal, and abuse of alcohol.

If you or a veteran's family member is experiencing re-entry challenges and you are in the Greater Rochester Area, call Veterans Outreach Center at 585-546-1081.

In Buffalo, New York, call Veterans Outreach Center at 716-424-1892 or call TOLL FREE: 1-866-906-VETS (8387).

In other areas, call the Veterans Crisis Line at 1-800-273-8255 or the National Suicide Prevention Lifeline at 1-800-273-TALK (8255).

Lynette Loomis

Acknowledgments

- **Thank you to the veterans and families** who volunteered to support this project and open their hearts and share their experiences in the hope it might help other men and women. Their names have been withheld to protect their privacy, with the exception of Marv Patterson, who said, "Use it!"

- **Amy P. Holtz** is the owner and head trainer of Hope 4 Your Canine, and founder and former President of Rudy's Rescue. She is currently in charge of intake, fosters and training. Rudy was hatched in 1995. Reach Amy at Hope4yourcanine.com.

- **Lynette Loomis,** a proud board member of long standing of Veterans Outreach Center, volunteered to help Hans write his story as a fundraiser for our residential programs. All proceeds benefit the veterans who have served us. Contact her at muddypawstories@rochester.rr.com

- **Meg Spencer** is an artist with a passion for veterans' issues and the wife of a 23-year Navy Veteran. Reach Meg at mmuller@rochester.rr.com.

- **Tom McShea** is a retired K9 Unit Sergeant, K9 Handler and K9 Trainer from the Monroe County Sheriff's Department (MCSD). He worked in the K9 Unit for 13 years and had a 23-year career with the MCSD. Tom is employed by Wegmans Food Markets in Asset Protection.

- **Brian Scanlon** is Vice President of Asset Protection for Wegmans Food Markets. He has been with Wegmans for 33 years. He is an ROTC Graduate from Eastern Kentucky University who was commissioned in the U.S. Army, serving four years in an overseas assignment.

- **Veterans Outreach Center (VOC) in Rochester, NY** was started by **Tom Cray**, **Bill Reddy** and **Tom Leckinger** more than 40 years ago. It is the nation's oldest free-standing veterans' agency, providing all services free of charge to veterans and their families. They began VOC during the Viet Nam era to help fellow veterans deal with their re-entry challenges. Over the past four-plus decades, veterans and their families and VOC volunteers and staff would agree that post-traumatic stress disorder (PTSD) is real. Richards and Otto Houses are VOC's residential programs, offering housing, counseling and education, education services, job training, and employment development. VOC is raising funds to buy and outfit a home for veterans who are women, many of whom have children. Hans arrived in December 2015 and lives happily with 28 veterans. www.veteransoutreachcenter.org

- **Wegmans Food Markets, Inc.** is a family-owned, 92-store supermarket chain with stores in New York, Pennsylvania, New Jersey, Virginia, Maryland and Massachusetts and is headquartered in Rochester, NY. Wegmans is recognized as an industry leader and innovator and is celebrating its 100th anniversary in 2016. Wegmans is known for its philanthropy to help strengthen local communities, and its financial support has made it possible for Hans to live at Veterans Outreach Center.

- **Starry Night Publishing.Com** uses new technology to offer publishing services at very competitive prices. Their services include cover design, compilation of text and graphics into appropriate files for eBooks or paperbacks, obtaining an ISBN number and copyright, making your book available through major online retailers, promoting your book through their online network, tracking your sales. All sales of this book will benefit Veterans Outreach Center and provide it with monthly royalty checks for U.S. and foreign sales. www.starrynightpublishing.com

Made in the USA
Middletown, DE
23 October 2016